John

To John. A reminder of your
Stay with us in Australia
Christmas 1981, with much love
from Uncle Tom & Aunty M.

To Marjorie Cotton.

D.W.D.

Copyright Text; A. B. Paterson
Illustrations: © Desmond Digby 1970
First published 1970 by William Collins (Australia) Ltd.
Tenth impression
Type set by Computype, Sydney
Printed by Dai Nippon Printing Co. (Hong Kong) Ltd.
ISBN 0 00 195010 x (HARDBACK)
ISBN 0 00 6614701 (PAPERBACK)

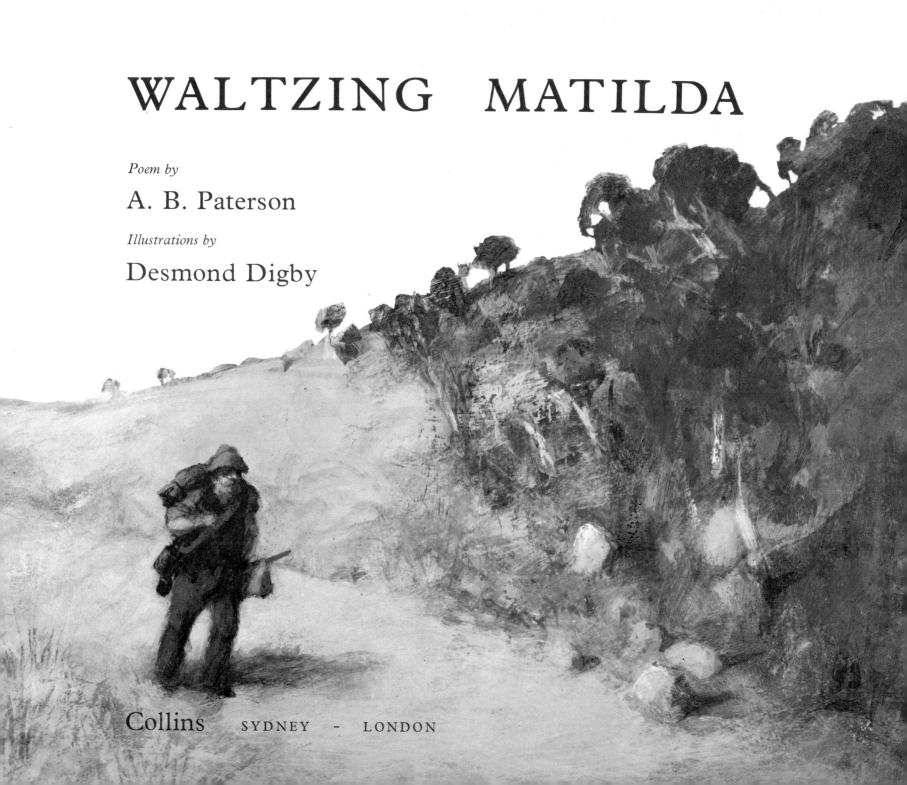

WALTZING MATILDA

Poem by

A. B. Paterson

Illustrations by

Desmond Digby

Collins SYDNEY - LONDON

Oh! There once was a swagman camped in a Billabong,

Under the shade of a Coolabah tree;

And he sang as he looked at his old billy boiling,

"Who'll come a-waltzing Matilda with me?"

Who'll come a-waltzing Matilda, my darling,
Who'll come a-waltzing Matilda with me?
Waltzing Matilda and leading a water-bag—
Who'll come a-waltzing Matilda with me?

Down came a jumbuck to drink at the water-hole,

Up jumped the swagman and grabbed him in glee;

And he sang as he stowed him away in his tucker-bag,

"You'll come a-waltzing Matilda with me!"

Who'll come a-waltzing Matilda, my darling,
Who'll come a-waltzing Matilda with me?
Waltzing Matilda and leading a water-bag—
Who'll come a-waltzing Matilda with me?

Down came the Squatter a-riding his thoroughbred;

Down came Policemen—one,

two

and three.

"Whose is the jumbuck you've got in your tucker-bag?

You'll come a-waltzing Matilda with me."

Who'll come a-waltzing Matilda, my darling,

Who'll come a-waltzing Matilda with me?

Waltzing Matilda and leading a water-bag—

Who'll come a-waltzing Matilda with me?

But the swagman, he up and he jumped in the water-hole,

Drowning himself by the Coolabah tree;

And his ghost may be heard as it sings in the billabong,

"Who'll come a-waltzing Matilda with me?"

GLOSSARY

BILLABONG: A backwater from an inland river, sometimes returning to it and sometimes ending in sand. Except in flood times it is usually a dried-up channel containing a series of pools or waterholes.

BILLY: A cylindrical tin pot with a lid and a wire handle used as a bushman's kettle.

COOLABAH TREE: A species of Eucalyptus, *E. microtheca*, common in the Australian inland where it grows along watercourses.

JUMBUCK: A sheep. From an Aboriginal word, the original meaning of which is obscure.

SQUATTER: Originally applied to a person who placed himself on public land without a licence, it was extended to describe a pastoralist who rented large tracts of Crown land for grazing and later to one who held his sheep run as freehold.

SWAGMAN: A man who, carrying his personal possessions in a bundle or SWAG, travels on foot in the country in search of casual or seasonal employment. A tramp.

WALTZING MATILDA: Carrying a swag; possibly a corruption of 'walking matilda'. 'Matilda' was a type of swag where the clothes and personal belongings were wrapped in a long blanket roll and tied towards each end like a Christmas cracker. It was carried around the neck with the loose ends falling down each side in front, one end clasped by the arm.